MW01119694

Fake News 101:

How to recognize fake news and avoid being fooled by it.

DANNY MURPHY

FakeNews101.info

FakeNewsToday.info

DannyMurphyAuthor.com

Table of Contents

Foreword

Danny Murphy and I have known each other for longer than I can remember. Although he only performed standup comedy for a few years, I was fortunate to see several of his performances. When he got on a rant, it was really something to behold. Other comedians said he was Kinison-esque. His bits on suicide whales, downsizing, and airline food were unforgettable. His impressions of Janis Joplin, Mike Tyson, and Jack Nicholson were mesmerizing.

He created his trivia game, Media Mayhem in the early 90s. The game got him over 50 guest spots on talk radio shows all over the country, including a few syndicated programs. He eventually got his own weekly radio show, the JokerJax Show. Listening to his humorous look back at the week's news was something I eagerly anticipated every Friday night.

Danny gave up performing comedy and took a regular job as a P.R. and Communications Manager with a social services agency. The good thing was that he kept on writing as a freelancer, and he put lots of his material together in ebooks. Humor 101 was based on his experience as a comedian, and it has become an indispensable resource to many public speakers.

In 2016, he ran for Congress in Florida's 4th District as a write-in candidate. Although he got more votes than anyone expected, he was not able to beat the well-funded Republican candidate. However, he did tell lots of jokes and touched lots of lives with his Make America Laugh Again campaign.

Danny has the ability to communicate with humor and he knows how to "find the funny" in most situations. He can also be surprisingly serious in his writing, depending on what is called for. He has been writing posts for The Fake News Review since 2016. This fine collection of his work is both enlightening and entertaining.

Jack O'Lanterni

Preface

I've been a news junkie since I was a boy. My first job in a suburb of Boston was delivering The Boston Globe, The Herald Traveler, and for a handful of discerning readers, the Record-American. My father worked in the Mailers' Union for the newspapers. When I was a teen, he got me a few shifts on Saturday nights putting the Sunday papers together at The Globe. That was back when the Sunday newspapers were gigantic.

I did well at writing in high school and I took writing classes in college. One of those courses was Magazine Feature Writing at the University of North Florida. Students in that class had to go through the process of writing and submitting four articles to magazines. One of mine got published, and it was a thrill to see my name in print. I went on to write book reviews for the Florida Times-Union and numerous articles that were published in excellent magazines like Onyx, The Wittenburg Door, and National Business Employment Weekly.

In the 90s a friend of mine who was in radio ran for Congress and I got involved with his campaign. During that time I read dozens of books about the media. I was trying to learn enough to become the logical pick for press secretary if my friend won. Unfortunately, he didn't win.

I had accumulated so much information that I felt like I had to do something with it. By that time, lots of Americans loathed the media, so I created a trivia game called Media Mayhem. I intended for it to be a fun way to learn about the media. Although the game didn't sell as well as I would have liked, I did manage to get on lots of talk radio shows throughout the country as a guest to talk about it.

I also got into comedy for a few years. I had an interesting schtick, but with three small children, going on the road to perform wasn't a good idea. You really can't progress much in comedy without going on the road for thirty weeks or more per year. Anyways, I got out of comedy and got a regular job doing communications work for a social services agency. I did their press releases, newsletters, website content, annual reports, and many other projects. The best part was pitching stories to various media, something I became very good at.

I've never stopped being a news junkie and I've continued to write for publication. Toward the end of 2016, it seemed to me that there would be a serious need for informative articles and blog posts to educate people about fake news. I wrote blog posts on topics like How to Spot Fake News, Pizzagate, Buzzfeed, Alternative Facts, and more.

To lighten things up, I also wrote fake news about fake news. Those posts include titles like Fake News Announces it will Develop a Code of Ethics, and a post about the fictitious Fakies Awards. I believe that humor and satire can be very effective for making points about serious subject matter.

This book is a compilation of many straight pieces - real news about fake news - along with a few satirical articles. In the back of the book, I've included interesting quotes pertaining to the media. There's also a glossary of terms used by the media that outsiders are not always familiar with.

Since the articles are stand-alone pieces, I recommend looking at the Table of Contents and clicking through to whatever appears to be most interesting. I sincerely hope that readers will find this material informative.

Danny Murphy

What is fake news?

"It comes at us from every quarter of the media—old and new—not just as satire but disguised as the real thing, secretly paid for by folks who want to remain in the shadows. And though much of it is clever, it's not all funny."
Robert Love, Columbia Journalism Review [1]

Although we appear to have entered a Golden Age of Fake News, fake stories have been passed off as news for a long time in the United States and throughout the world. On December 28, 1917, the New York Evening Mail presented readers with one of the greatest fake news stories up to that time. "A Neglected Anniversary" by H.L. Mencken was a totally fake history of the bathtub. It may be hard for people to believe that an article about bathtub history could go viral, but it did.

Flashing forward to 1980, Janet Cooke wrote an article for the Washington Post about an 8-year-old heroin addict named Jimmy. The story, which was titled "Jimmy's World," was heart-breaking. After Cooke won a Pulitzer Prize, people wanted to locate Jimmy so they could help the lad. Unfortunately, there was no Jimmy. Janet had cooked the whole story up.

Stephen Glass was another "journalist" who found his way to fortune, fame, and infamy by making things up. He wrote mostly for The New Republic where he became an associate editor by the age of twenty-five. Forbes.com outed him in May of 1998. The article was titled "Lies, Damn Lies and Fiction" by Adam L. Penenberg.

In 2003, The New York Times disclosed that award-winning reporter Jayson Blair had been a plagiarist and a frequent fabricator. In his articles, he had a bad habit of inserting quotes from interviews that never took place. According to The Times, there were problems in "at least 36 of the 73 articles Mr. Blair wrote since he started getting national reporting assignments."

---

1. Robert Love, Before Jon Stewart, Columbia Journalism Review, March/April 2007, **http://archives.cjr.org/feature/before_jon_stewart.php**

These are but a few examples of fake news in which journalists intentionally misled consumers of the news. Sometimes the media also report fake stories unwittingly. In October of 2009, the Balloon Boy captivated audiences as he reportedly floated through the sky in a balloon. Reporters and TV viewers alike ate the story up. It turned out that Falcon Heene had never even left the ground. He had been safe at home the whole time. It turned out that his parents had pulled off one of the greatest hoaxes in modern history.

Since the turn of the millennium, fake news has been evolving at an accelerated pace. Not so long ago, tabloids including The Weekly World News, which specialized in fake news, could be readily found in many grocery stores. Fake news in print is not as common as it once was, although we still see it occasionally in newspapers and magazines. Now most of the fake news is on the internet.

The Onion, which bills itself as America's Finest News Source, is the most well-known publisher of fake news, but there are dozens of other online magazines cranking it out. With some websites, like The Onion, it's clear that the stories presented are satirical. Nevertheless, there are people who believe the articles. Other websites do a very good job of looking legitimate, and for many readers it is easy to believe the articles. For many readers, it has become difficult to distinguish what's real and what's not.

Fake News 101 will help readers to recognize various types of fake news. It also presents information on how fake news operates, with examples. Aside from disconnecting and finding a wireless cave to live in, there's probably no way to avoid fake news completely. However, it is possible to avoid being fooled by fake news. The objective of Fake News 101 is to help people to do exactly that.

Look, up in the sky. Is it a bird? Is it a plane? No! It's the Balloon Boy riding high once again!

Fake Hysteria: Orson Welles and the War of the Worlds

Like many writers, I sometimes do other work to make ends meet. One of the jobs I've had involved reviewing short written answers to test questions about a designated reading. The students were eleventh graders and one of the readings was about Orson Welles' famous War of the Worlds broadcast on Mercury Theatre on the Air.

On his show, Orson Welles presented audiences with dramatizations of various novels. On October 30, 1938, the selection was War of the Worlds, an 1898 novel by H.G. Wells. The novel was adapted to depict a live invasion of Grover Mills, New Jersey, by hostile Martians. According to lore, the broadcast sent millions of Americans into a panic.

However, that lore has been debunked. W. Joseph Campbell, a professor at American University, wrote about War of the Worlds in his book, **Getting It Wrong: Debunking the Greatest Myths in American Journalism.** "In short, the notion that the War of the Worlds program sent untold thousands of people into the streets in panic is a media-driven myth that offers a deceptive message about the power radio wielded over listeners in its early days and, more broadly, about the media's potential to sow fright, panic, and alarm," he wrote.[2]

Jefferson Pooley and Michael J. Socolow of Slate Magazine also wrote an informative article about The Myth of the War of the Worlds Panic. "How did the story of panicked listeners begin?" they asked. "Blame America's newspapers. Radio had siphoned off advertising revenue from print during the Depression, badly damaging the newspaper industry. So the papers seized the opportunity presented by Welles' program to discredit radio as a source of news. The newspaper industry sensationalized the panic to prove to advertisers, and regulators, that radio management was irresponsible and not to be trusted." The article appeared in Slate on October 28th, 2013.

---

2. W. Joseph Campbell, Getting It Wrong, Fright beyond Measure, University of California Press, page 27

http://www.slate.com/articles/arts/history/2013/10/orson_welles_war_o f_the_worlds_panic_myth_the_infamous_radio_broadcast_did.html

Getting back to those eleventh graders, for their test they read an essay about the War of the Worlds which appeared to be authoritative. Then many of the students opined that with the various media now available to everyone through the internet, it would be impossible for anyone to fool people the way many supposedly were fooled by the War of the Worlds broadcast in 1938.

Many of the students seemed to think that the availability of information from numerous sources ensures that readers and viewers of the news will be able to make better evaluations of stories in the news. The problem is that most people don't access all of the information available to them on any given subject. Who has the time for that?

There's now so much information and opinion available on most subjects that it would be challenging to look at all of the pertinent media with which one generally agrees. People who lean to the political right gravitate toward publishers that support that perspective. Those include Fox News, National Review, Weekly Standard, Newsmax, Breitbart, InfoWars, and others, depending on how far to the right a person leans. Likewise, people who lean to the left can find plenty of what they agree with on CNN, MSNBC, The Daily Beast, Occupy Democrats, Mother Jones and many other fine news outlets.

Having information from many sources can help consumers of the news, but only if they look at lots of it and know how to make sense of it all. In 1938, following the War of the Worlds broadcast, when stories about panic in the streets were appearing in lots of newspapers, people believed them. The storyline was so pervasive that intelligent people believe it to this day. (I believed it right up to the day I began digging a bit for information for this article.)

Nevertheless, in spite of the story being covered very similarly in many places, it, apparently, was not true. Today, even though we have many more sources of information available to us than ever before, our skills at evaluating what we are consuming may not be much better than those of the people who believed the War of the Worlds myth.

Fake News is here to stay!

Read all about it.

Note: This is the unedited version of a letter to the editor from Danny Murphy that appeared in the Florida Times-Union on January 1, 2017.

Fake news isn't going away. The folks who consume it just love the stuff! More importantly, producers of fake news and advertisers alike are making money from it.

Fake news producers cater to people who believe what they want to believe, meaning most people. When presented with a story that precisely fits a person's belief system, he or she tends to believe it.

Still, there are some people who prefer not to be fooled. A great deal of the fake news going around is satire. Recognizing satirical fake news isn't hard. If a story is from The Onion or The Daily Currant, it's certainly fake and potentially very funny.

For stories from elsewhere that seem outrageous or unlikely, clicking through to the websites where they first appeared can be revealing. If the About page mentions satire and/or entertainment, the stories are probably all fake.

If the names of the reporters or the characters in the stories seem like made up names, they probably are. The biggest key to not being fooled by fake news is to set aside biases and ask yourself whether a story is likely to be true, regardless of how much you might like it to be true.

DANNY MURPHY

Not all fake news is created equally.

There are several varieties of fake news. Here are two of the most common forms.

Satire

The most prevalent and obvious type of fake news is satirical fake news. This includes everything from material in The Onion, to Weekend Update on Saturday Night Live, to The Daily Show with Trevor Noah. The emphasis is on humor and getting laughs. Sometimes people are not aware that they're reading or watching satire. Some people take satire completely seriously. Also, there are people who don't understand what satire is or how it works through irony, exaggeration, and other methods.

Good satire is funny, although not usually to everybody. People generally don't like it when they realize they or their beliefs are being made fun of. Also, there's generally a point to good satire. In many cases, satire can be more effective for getting a message across than trying to be persuasive in a straightforward manner. People enjoy laughing. If they're laughing, they're listening and processing what they're hearing.

Fabrication

People who read and watch the news don't always realize how tedious and time-consuming it is to put a story together. It involves research, tracking down people who may not want to be cooperative, interviews, writing, fact-checking, rewriting, editing, and probably more rewriting. In addition, media professionals are being asked to do more than ever before. Instead of covering one primary beat, a reporter may now be called upon to cover two or three or more areas.

A reporter may also have to take pictures, shoot video, and engage with subscribers on social media. It's not as easy as many people who have never done it might think. Rather than deal with those challenges day after day, some reporters simply make things up. Quotes, characters, whatever. Making things up is much more efficient for a busy reporter than producing

12

a real story, doing real interviews, and digging beneath the surface.

Another type of fabrication that sometimes goes on is when media professionals massage the available information to suit a specific agenda. Video and audio can be edited in ways that distort what happened. Although journalists are supposed to be objective in their reporting, they do have biases, like other people, and sometimes those biases seep into their work. It's human nature. That appears to have been the case in the leadup to the election of 2016 when it was widely reported that Donald Trump didn't stand a chance of winning.

Yet another type of fabrication is when people lie to the media. They do this to get attention, or to promote their own agendas, or both. Unfortunately, busy media professionals sometimes believe lies far too easily. It's easier to simply believe what you're being told than to dig deeper for the truth.

The following are interesting examples.

Gay pastor admits he faked homophobic slur on Whole Foods cake. Washington Post.

https://www.washingtonpost.com/news/acts-of-faith/wp/2016/05/16/gay-pastor-admits-he-faked-homophobic-slur-on-whole-foods-cake/?utm_term=.6dd41590c265

6 types of misinformation circulated this election season. Columbia Journalism Review.

http://www.cjr.org/tow_center/6_types_election_fake_news.php

Malkin: Liberal Media's Manufactured Narratives Are the Definition of Fake News. Fox News.

http://insider.foxnews.com/2016/12/05/michelle-malkin-donald-trump-fake-news-cnn-media-dnc-debates

BuzzFeed Caught Citing Fake Data In Its 'Fake News Won The Election For Trump' Argument. Daily Caller.

http://dailycaller.com/2016/12/09/buzzfeed-caught-citing-fake-data-in-its-fake-news-won-the-election-for-trump-argument-again/#ixzz4SR9eizDt

Satire and Fake News

"You can fool all the people some of the time, and some of the people all the time, but you cannot fool all the people all the time." Abraham Lincoln

According to Wikipedia, satire is a genre of literature, and sometimes graphic and performing arts, in which vices, follies, abuses, and shortcomings are held up to ridicule, ideally with the intent of shaming individuals, corporations, government, or society itself into improvement.

The United States has had a rich tradition of satire. Some of the country's most notable satirists have been Ben Franklin, Mark Twain, and Will Rogers. The late Art Buchwald and P.J. O'Rourke are two of our more recent satirists. Television shows like Saturday Night Live, The Daily Show, and many others present satire as well. Mad Magazine, Cracked, and National Lampoon have all put a great deal of satire into print. The Wittenburg Door, which published some of my satire, billed itself as "The world's pretty much only religious satire magazine."

Satire is more complicated than a straightforward piece of writing or video. Like good jokes, satire begins with a premise, an underlying idea. For example, during the Presidential campaign of 2016, two premises that were used over and over were that Donald Trump didn't have the temperament to be President and Hillary Clinton was a liar. More often than not, satire is a humorous way of making the point of the premise, whatever the premise may be.

Satire is one of the most prevalent forms of fake news on the internet. Many of the popular memes that circulate on the internet are satirical. The Onion, The Daily Currant, and many other websites specialize in satire. Many consumers of news love good satire. However, people who read or view satire don't always see things the same way.

Here are some of the ways that people react to satirical material.

- They get the joke, agree with the premise, and get a good laugh out of it.

- They get the joke, disagree with the premise, and get upset about it.

- They may not get the joke and wonder why other people are laughing. That's an uncomfortable feeling for most people.

- They may not understand what satire is and take whatever they're reading or seeing at face value. This is happening with alarming frequency and it's the main reason I'm preparing to release a new book titled Remedial Satire. It's being published by Doublespeak Books and it should be in bookstores by April 1st.

When people realize that they've been made the butt of a joke, they generally aren't happy about it. For example, President Trump hasn't been very pleased with the way Alec Baldwin has been parodying him on Saturday Night Live.

When you read a piece of satire, there are usually a few clues to indicate that it is satire. Funky names and preposterous statements may be indicators that a piece of work is satire.

Fake news websites that specialize in satire.

Although many people continue to take the fake news bait, determining whether a website is fake or not is frequently as easy as looking at the About page. This is especially true for websites that deal in satire. Here are several examples.

The Onion

"The Onion is the world's leading news publication, offering highly acclaimed, universally revered coverage of breaking national, international, and local news events. Rising from its humble beginnings as a print newspaper in 1765, *The Onion* now enjoys a daily readership of 4.3 trillion and has grown into the single most powerful and influential organization in human history... *The Onion* supports more than 350,000 full- and part-time journalism jobs in its numerous news bureaus and manual labor camps."

Funny stuff! No intelligent person could read that and think it was serious.

News Biscuit: the news before it happens.

"NewsBiscuit was launched by John O'Farrell in September 2006 with the noble aims of eradicating global poverty, creating a lasting peace in the Middle East and providing a daily dose of humour to bored people at work. And in many respects we have already achieved so much more."

Like The Onion's about page, this is very tongue-in-cheek.

The Enduring Vision

"The Enduring Vision is an award-winning satirical webpage. It has been around in some form or another since the dawn of man; early forms of the site's logo and layout have been discovered in caves where human ancestors were known to live. This makes The Enduring Vision the original news satire publication, even though now there are about 100 million others."

Again, funny.

Real News Right Now

"R. Hobbus J.D. is an internationally acclaimed independent investigative journalist specializing in international politics, health, business, science, conflict resolution, history, geography, mathematics, social issues, feminism, space travel, civil rights, human rights, animal rights, fashion, film, astronomy, classic literature, religion, biology, paranormal activity, the occult, physics, psychology, and creative writing... He has received numerous awards for his work including the prestigious Stephen Glass Distinction in Journalistic Integrity (2011), The Oscar Mayer Award for Journalistic Excellence (2003), three Nobel Peace Prize nominations, one Pulitzer in Investigative Reporting (1998), and two Pulitzer Prizes in Commentary (1996, 2008). He resides comfortably in his modest home overlooking the coast of Nantucket surrounded by his wife and twelve cats."

CAP News

Although CAP News doesn't have an about page, at the very bottom of the webpages it clearly says, "All material is satire."

Some satirical websites have highly visible slogans at the tops of the pages that tell readers what they're in for.

News Mutiny: Satire for the wise. News for the dumb.

Fake News Review: Real news about fake news! Fake News about fake news!

So, if you find yourself reading something and you wonder whether it's real or fake, take a look at the About page and you'll probably be able to figure it out.

Wit Privilege and America's War on the Witless

Note: This article first appeared on June 4, 2015, in The American Thinker. It's an example of satirical fake news.

"Against the assault of laughter, nothing can stand." Mark Twain

Wit is not always a laughing matter. For example, the Sons of Liberty used their wits to pull off one of the most memorable practical jokes in history at the Boston Tea Party. Also, Ben Franklin disseminated and popularized his philosophy through his bestseller, *Poor Richard's Almanac.* His witty one-liners are quoted to this day by people who've never even heard of the book.

Wit privilege refers to societal privileges that benefit witty people in ways that are unavailable to the witless. It continues to be a potent force in the United States. The witty elite use jokes and anecdotes to win elections, spread ideologies, and market their services and wares. All too often, the witless are the butts of the jokes. They are at a severe disadvantage in virtually every area of their sad lives.

Witty people are more likeable, more popular, and have greater social status. They tend to be cheerful, and they receive more respect and better service across the board. From bankers to beauticians, from the police to pediatricians, from clerks to computer techs, people who provide services of any kind prefer to do business with funny people rather than the grumpy.

The witty are also considered more attractive than the witless. That's why comedians never have problems finding spouses, or second, or third, or fourth spouses. A review of personal ads will inevitably show that the most desired trait for a potential date is a good sense of humor. Nobody writes personal ads like this: "Seeking somber person to engage in serious conversation. Must not giggle."

Funny folks have greater freedom of expression. In America, when you're funny people listen. The ability to tell a joke can make the difference between being heard and being ignored. Funny videos are shared far more often than serious ones. In the entertainment business, people who can make others laugh get more opportunities and are treated better than the humor-impaired.

The disparities between the witty and the witless are evident in the business world as well. A properly delivered punchline can help a person land a job or seal a deal. Jokes are also frequently used by the powerful to silence the witless. The laughter emanating from corner offices may sound jovial, but it also reminds the peons in the cubicles of who is in charge.

Disparities due to wit privilege are rampant in healthcare. People who know how to tell jokes and enjoy a good laugh live happier and healthier lives. The witty are able to handle stress and anxiety better than the witless. Laughter is widely regarded as the best medicine, and the witty get it for free. The primary reason comedy isn't part of healthcare is that they want to keep it to themselves. Meanwhile, people who suffer from humor deficiency pay exorbitant amounts for the prescription and non-prescription drugs they need just to get through the day.

Witty people take their unearned benefits for granted. When confronted about wit privilege, they deny that it exists or say that it's not their fault they were born funny. Furthermore, they have no comprehension of how different their lives would be if they ever lost their sense of humor and had to experience horrors like these:

- The realization, after they've delivered a punchline, that they've omitted a critical part of the setup.

- The inability to produce suitable and timely responses to offensive remarks or insults.

- Dreaded sympathy laughter due to poor comedic timing.

The roots of wit privilege go all the way back to William Shakespeare. In Othello, the bard wrote, "They laugh that win."

Little has changed. Renowned neurohumorist Karyn Buxman proclaims, "Humor is power."

Wit privilege has had a profound and disturbing influence in the United States throughout the country's history. It is deplorable that humorous people have advantages over people who are not funny and who may never become funny. People born witless are human beings entitled to the same freedoms and opportunities as the witty.

The longstanding and systemic abuses of power enabled through wit privilege are a form of discrimination which must be addressed. In the interest of fairness and decency, if an equitable solution cannot be found, the laughter must stop.

False Reports of Celebrity Deaths

"Reports of my death have been greatly exaggerated." Mark Twain

Real deaths of celebrities are usually big news. Because of that, one of the most frequent types of fake news is false reports of celebrity deaths. Fake news about celebrity deaths can generate lots of web traffic and revenue for the purveyors of fake news. These reports are completely fabricated and are not merely mistakes in reporting. They are designed for one thing, and that is to generate clicks and produce revenue for the producers.

The list of celebrities who have passed away according to fake news is practically endless. They include Robert Redford, Carlos Santana, Paul McCartney, Jackie Chan, Cher, Macauly Culkin, Eminem, Tom Hanks, Miley Cyrus, Tom Cruise, Mark-Paul Gosselaar, Judd Nelson, Harrison Ford, Charlie Sheen, Paris Hilton, Jaden Smith, Jack Black, Sylvester Stallone, Hugh Hefner, Lady Gaga, Morgan Freeman, Jeff Goldblum, Tony Danza, Justin Bieber, Eddie Murphy, Russell Crowe, Reba McEntire, Adam Sandler, Tiger Woods, Willie Nelson, and many others. Some celebrities die over and over on the internet, like a character on Southpark.

Digiday published a good article by Lucia Mose on "How celebrity death hoaxes power fake news." In the article, Mose wrote, "The fake stories follow a loose pattern: Often coming from sites with legit-sounding names like Msmbc.co and Nbctoday.co, the stories tend to focus on young, popular celebrities with many fans who would be shocked by their premature death, causing a burst of traffic to the site, which is paid for with programmatically served ads."

When people who are fans of the famous hear of the death of an idol, it's very normal to click on a link to see what's going on. It seems to be an involuntary response, as if they can't help themselves.

Although it doesn't seem particularly harmful to click through on a report of a celebrity's death, this type of fake news is an excellent way to spread viruses. A blog post by Appriver breaks down how one of these virus campaigns worked.

Fake Headlines of Celebrity Death Leads to Malware Infection.

https://blog.appriver.com/2010/08/fake-headlines-of-celebrity-death-leads-to-malware-infection/

Beware! Clicking on links about celebrity deaths can lead to malware including scareware or ransomware. AOL posted an informative article about that.

Scamwatch: Celebrity Death Fraud.

http://www.aol.co.uk/money/2017/03/11/scamwatch-celebrity-death-fraud/

Malicious Fake News

Some fake news is very malicious. For example, a photo that circulated in April of 2017 showed Donald Trump's backside as he was walking on a golf course. The digitally altered photo showed a brown stain on his white pants. That was supposedly from an "accident" involving diarrhea. The photo by itself didn't get much attention, but when a website added a story to it, it got into much wider circulation. Erica Abbott wrote an informative article about the incident in **Business2Community**.

http://www.business2community.com/government-politics/photo-donald-trump-getting-diarrhea-golf-course-digital-fake-01817683#lEYqBlVCMvAdYCr5.97

A similarly distasteful photo of Hillary Clinton circulated as a meme while she was on the campaign trail in May of 2016. The meme referred to "Incontinent Hillary." Snopes reported that the original photo was taken in 1996 and was digitally altered for the meme.

http://www.snopes.com/photograph-incontinent-hillary-clinton/

This is the level to which some producers of fake news will stoop in order to get clicks, earn revenue, and/or promote their causes. There are plenty of internet surfers who want to believe the very worst about politicians and other celebrities they don't like. They are the folks who make memes like these profitable to the producers.

In December of 2017, after Pizzagate, Hillary Clinton spoke out about fake news. "The epidemic of malicious fake news and fake propaganda that flooded social media over the past year, it's now clear that so-called fake news can have real-world consequences," she said. Whether or not a person agrees with Clinton most of the time, what she said there was true.

Malicious fake news is also being used for social engineering by Advanced Persistent Threat (APT) groups. These groups are highly sophisticated and some have been very successful at distributing malware throughout the world. The tools of their trade include fake news which they use as lures to entice people to click.

"Cyber adversaries tailor spear phishing and malvertising lures to stimulate cyber-hygienically inept users' insatiable need to 'click' on everything and anything that momentarily ensnares their attention. Lures range in complexity from precise, error-free custom tailored spear-phishing emails that leverage the target's LinkedIn profile, to typo-filled mass-spam... Social engineering remains the dominant attack vector used by sophisticated and unsophisticated cyber adversaries alike." James Scott, Senior Fellow at the **Institute for Critical Infrastructure Technology.**[3]

So, when you see a headline/link that you feel like you simply must click on, think twice. Someone out there may be trying to use you to get access to your organization's IT systems.

---

3. James Scott, Fake News is Old News for Nation State and Mercenary APTs, Institute for Critical Infrastructure Technologies. (http://icitech.org/fake-news-is-nothing-new-for-nation-state-and-mercenary-apts/)

Propaganda for
War and Peace

"The first casualty when war comes is truth." Hiram W Johnson. *This quote is also sometimes attributed to the Greek dramatist Aeschylus.*

It's not easy to get Americans to support war. In 1917, President Woodrow Wilson appointed journalist George Creel as Chairman of the new Committee for Public Information. In an article for The American Experience, Nicholas Cull wrote, "For two years, he rallied the American public to the cause of war and sold the globe a vision of America and President Wilson's plans for a world order. He was a controversial figure in wartime Washington, but his efforts changed the ideological landscape at home and abroad, and many of the methods and approaches he pioneered became a standard part of U.S. statecraft." [4]

Near the beginning of the 21st century, George W. Bush and his team made the case for war in Iraq based primarily on intelligence reports that the regime in Iraq was hiding weapons of mass destruction. The war was undertaken and Saddam Hussein was captured. However, the evidence of WMDs was not as strong as the pre-war intelligence indicated.

Fake news can also be used to make the case for peace. In 1938 Neville Chamberlin, the British Prime Minister, gave a speech titled "Peace for Our Time." He said, "My good friends, for the second time in our history, a British Prime Minister has returned from Germany bringing peace with honor." A year later, Germany invaded Poland. Shortly after that, Britain and France declared war on Germany.

---

4. Nicolas Cull, Master of American Propaganda, American Experience, **http://www.pbs.org/wgbh/americanexperience/features/the-great-war-master-of-american-propaganda/**

Similarly, and much more recently, the Obama team assured Americans that all chemical weapons were removed from Syria and everything was going to be just fine. In an interview with NPR (in January, 2017, former National Security Adviser Susan Rice said, "We were able to find a solution that didn't necessitate the use of force that actually removed the chemical weapons that were known from Syria, in a way that the use of force would never have accomplished." As many Syrians found out firsthand, and as observers throughout the world saw in April of 2017, Syria still had a stockpile of chemical weapons.

http://www.npr.org/sections/parallels/2017/01/16/510047606/obama-adviser-susan-rice-cites-syrian-war-as-biggest-disappointment)

This wasn't Susan Rice's first time disseminating fake news. Following the deadly attack on Ambassador Chris Stevens and three other Americans in Benghazi, Rice went on numerous TV news shows to inform viewers that the attack was the result of a mob crazed by the airing of a low budget movie that didn't portray The Prophet in a good light. Even though that tall tale was later discredited, it proved that fake news can be very effective as a temporary distraction.

Then came Secretary of State Clinton's infamous question, "What difference does it make?" It is obvious to most people that the primary purpose of getting to the truth about the deaths of four Americans in Benghazi was to formulate policies for avoiding similar attacks in the future. Clinton's fake question was accompanied by fake outrage.

In April of 2017, The Weekly Standard published an excellent article about some of these issues.

Are Syria's Chemical Weapons Iraq's Missing WMD? Obama's Director of Intelligence Thought So.

http://www.weeklystandard.com/are-syrias-chemical-weapons-iraqs-missing-wmd-obamas-director-of-intelligence-thought-so./article/2007610

How to spot fake news.

"There's a sucker born every minute." Most frequently attributed to P.T. Barnum.

"We won't get fooled again." Pete Townsend

Most people have been suckers at least once or twice in their lives.
For example, before writing this article, I always thought that P.T. Barnum
was the originator of the oft-quoted line about suckers. Alas, it appears that
I took too much for granted.

According to Garson O'Toole, **Quote Investigator**, "The two expressions
'there's a fool born every minute' and 'there's a sucker born every minute'
both had anonymous attributions initially. Over time they were reassigned
to prominent individuals of the time period. However, only the fame of
P.T. Barnum has endured. Today, the phrase 'there's a sucker born every
minute' is often ascribed to him. Yet, support for this ascription is very
weak. Citations occurred at the very end of his life and after his death." [5]

**Speaking of fools and suckers, many people are now being fooled by
fake news.** Another saying that many people are familiar with asserts that if
something sounds too good to be true, it probably is. I have not tracked
down the exact origin of that line, but it appears that it may only go back
fifty years or so. In any case, when it comes to fake news, I would suggest
that if people come across news that's hard to believe, it might not be true.
Complicating matters, when news is very easy to believe, it cold be fake
news as well.

Producers of fake news make money from people clicking on links.
They have algorithms to figure out what people will click on. Before the
election, an outrageous story about Donald Trump or anyone in his family
could appeal to a certain audience. That will probably go on for as long as
he is in office. Likewise, for a different audience, crazy stories about Hillary
Clinton or Bill Clinton could work.

---

5. Garson O'Toole, There's a Sucker Born Every Minute, Quote Investigator,
http://quoteinvestigator.com/2014/04/11/fool-born/

Facts and truth don't matter to producers of fake news. All that matters to them is how many revenue producing clicks a story will get. There is a ton of fake news going around and it is meticulously tailored to motivate people to click.

For example, there have been numerous stories about how insanely stupid Sarah Palin is. One item that made the rounds had Palin talking about the way Jesus celebrated Easter. One of the comments to the story said, "You can't make this stuff up." Actually, that story was made up. The source was The Daily Currant, which on its About page identifies itself as, "an English language online satirical newspaper that covers global politics, business, technology, entertainment, science, health and media." Still, many people believed the story and shared it because they wanted to believe it and they wanted others to believe as well.

So, how can Joe or Jodie Sixpack spot fake news so that he, or she, is not sucked in by it?

First, if it's from The Onion or The Daily Currant, it's fake and potentially very funny. If it's from somewhere else, click through to the website and look at the About page. If they mention satire, entertainment, etc., it's fake. Look over other stories on the website. If some of them seem too stupid to be true, all of their stories may be fake. If the names of the reporters seem like made up names, they are probably pseudonyms.

Try to set aside your biases long enough to ask whether a the story is likely to be true. Many people are fooled because fake news stories they are consuming cater to their biases. If you're concerned about the news you're consuming, here are a few good articles you might like to check out.

How to Spot Fake News. FactCheck.org

http://www.factcheck.org/2016/11/how-to-spot-fake-news/

Snopes' Field Guide to Fake News Sites and Hoax Purveyors

http://www.snopes.com/2016/01/14/fake-news-sites/

How To Recognize A Fake News Story. Huffington Post

http://www.huffingtonpost.com/entry/fake-news-guide-facebook_us_5831c6aae4b058ce7aaba169

Two words that indicate a news story might be fake news.

In days of yore, publishers and editors didn't put stories on the air or into print until they had enough of the facts to support the storyline. Sometimes in the race to break a story ahead of the competition, they got a little ahead of themselves. When they did, they sometimes printed or aired material that was not accurate and had to be retracted or corrected. Since reputations are important to news organizations, they avoided making mistakes as much as possible.

Now, to stay ahead of other outlets, some news organizations go with material that hasn't yet been fleshed out. Understanding a few code words can help consumers to recognize when a story might, possibly, potentially be fake news. For example, James Rosen of Fox News wrote a story on March 23rd, 2017, with the following provocative title.

Potential 'smoking gun' showing Obama administration spied on Trump team, source says.

http://www.foxnews.com/politics/2017/03/23/potential-smoking-gun-showing-obama-administration-spied-on-trump-team-source-says.html

A potential smoking gun? How exciting! That is, until one realizes that when a reporter talks about a potential smoking gun, he or she doesn't have a smoking gun and there may not be a smoking gun at all. In my opinion, a story about a potential smoking gun is only potentially a story. However, that was real enough for Sean Hannity to interview James Rosen about the potential smoking gun.

It was also real enough for The Blaze, Breitbart, and other organizations that lean to the right to repeat the story. After March 23rd, evidence dribbled out that supports the original piece. For consumers of news, it may have been better to wait till the smoking gun was evident than to move forward with a potential story.

That same day, March 23rd, there was a similar incident originating from the left. Manu Raju and Theodore Schleifer of CNN reported on a story with this headline.

Schiff: New evidence shows possible Trump-Russia collusion.

http://www.cnn.com/2017/03/23/politics/adam-schiff-trump-russia-grand-jury/index.html

When reporters write about possible collusion, the possibility remains that the evidence may not support the headline. In my opinion, a news item about possible collusion is really only a potential news story. Consumers would be better off if CNN had waited till they had something real to present instead of going ahead with a story about possible collusion. This is especially true since there appear to be lots of potential stories related to possible collusion that have not yet been fleshed out completely.

Unfortunately, potential and possible stories are here and they're not going away. News stories that prominently feature the words possible and potential may or may not be real. News consumers should take such stories with a large grain of salt.

2017 is the Year of the Leak

Throughout the election season of 2016 and beyond, more information has been leaked from various government agencies than ever before. Information leaks aren't new. They have been used in a variety of ways for decades.

Deep Throat was the code name for one of the most famous leakers of them all. Deep Throat leaked information about the Watergate break-in and cover-up to Bob Woodward and Carl Bernstein of the Washington Post. The stories that came out resulted in the resignation of President Richard Nixon.

In 2005, reports came out that W. Mark Felt, who was an assistant director at the FBI in the 70s, was Deep Throat. Since employees of the FBI are not supposed to leak government secrets, it's no wonder that Felt preferred not to be identified.

What is a leak?

According to Wikipedia, a leak is a way (usually an opening) for fluid to escape a container or fluid-containing system, such as a tank or a ship's hull, through which the contents of the container can escape or outside matter can enter the container. Leaks are usually unintended and therefore undesired.

The word leak also applies to information which is intended to be kept secret but which gets out anyways. Edward Snowden leaked lots of information. Then he left the country. More recently, someone leaked wiretapped information about Michael Flynn's communications with the Russian ambassador. Flynn resigned soon thereafter. And, of course, Wikileaks has been up to lots of leaking mischief, releasing tons of CIA files.

How are leaks used and abused?

Two of the biggest reasons people leak information are to attack an adversary and/or to promote some agenda. Some who leak information do it out of principle. They see something that's not right and they believe that if enough people find out, the result will be positive change. Others leak information as a means of making life more difficult for an enemy. Most leakers probably do it for some combination of reasons.

Why do people prefer to stay anonymous?

People who leak information have lives, like everyone else. The fallout that can come from a juicy leak can be very disruptive. If possible, leakers would like to go on with their lives with as little disruption as possible, unless, of course there's some potential for a book deal and there's not much chance of getting killed over the leak.

For some people, leaking information can result in the loss of a good livelihood. Business people who leak information may run the risk of no longer being trusted by folks they have been associated with. Also, people who leak classified information don't want their names out there because they would prefer to avoid getting arrested and going to prison.

Leaks in 2017

In the first quarter of 2017 alone, it appeared that more federal employees were leaking information to the press than those who were not. At the beginning of March, Team Trump came up with plans to plug the leaks emanating from the White House. Those plans were leaked almost immediately to the media.

The Hill: Trump team's push to stop leaks quickly leaks to press.

http://thehill.com/homenews/administration/322155-trump-teams-push-to-stop-leaks-quickly-leaks-to-press

Time: White House Collected Cell Phones to Crack Down on Leaks. Then That Leaked.

http://time.com/4685574/sean-spicer-cell-phone-leak-crack-down/

Meanwhile, some in the media are making the case that leaks are not un-American and that they're not likely to stop anytime soon.

L.A. Times: Is it really 'un-American' to leak news to the press?

http://www.latimes.com/politics/washington/la-na-essential-washington-updates-is-it-really-un-american-to-leak-news-1487180265-htmlstory.html

Chicago Tribune: Donald Trump can't stop government leaks

http://www.chicagotribune.com/news/opinion/commentary/ct-trump-authoritarian-leaks-investigation-20170224-story.html

Politico: Why the Leaks Won't Stop - POLITICO Magazine.

http://www.politico.com/magazine/story/2017/02/why-the-leaks-wont-stop-214824

Alternative Facts and the Rise of Fake News

"We are the ones that determine what people's attitudes are. It's in our hands." Ted Turner

Although some people deny that the media can control the way they think, it would be hard to make the case that the media don't affect what we think about. Editors and producers decide which stories appear at the top of the hour or on the front page. They also decide which stories are worthy of coverage and which can be completely ignored.

Reporters have a hand in deciding who to interview and what questions to ask. They decide which opinions merit inclusion in stories and which do not. They decide which sources of information are trustworthy and which are not. Then they put stories together in the way that seems most logical to them. One ever-present objective is to do the job in such a way that the boss is happy with it.

Video editors look at the footage available to them and decide what the story is, from beginning, to middle, to end. They decide which portions will be best for telling the story. The power to leave one thing in and take others out is tremendous. One of the key considerations for news video is that it's interesting to look at. Stories with no interesting footage don't make producers happy. A marginal story which comes with great footage will frequently be chosen over a substantial story with lousy footage.

When I was pitching stories for a non-profit, there were several events per year - seminars, workshops, etc. - that my bosses wanted to get covered on local TV. Time after time, I had to explain that even though the subject was utterly fascinating, talking heads would not get coverage unless one of the talking heads was a celebrity or the event took place on a very slow news day.

I always knew that unless I could provide producers, editors, and reporters with what they needed, there was no point in pitching anything to them. People in the media are usually in a hurry and working to get things done before a deadline. If I put the resources together for them, that would make their jobs easier and get me a step closer to getting the kind of coverage I was looking for. For print stories, I even supplied pictures so the editors wouldn't have to send a photographer.

Why do protestors get covered more than speakers at conferences? Because they can be relied upon for interesting footage. Why did Donald Trump get more coverage than other candidates while he was campaigning? Because the media could always count on him to say something interesting and/or controversial.

It doesn't seem possible that all of the dubious statements and alternative facts coming out of Team Trump could be unintentional. They may be cranking some of it out with the objective of distracting the media, sending reporters on wild goose chases that lead to stories that aren't very significant. Politicians tell lies. So do their press secretaries and other hired hands. The big surprise is that anyone is surprised by that.

Buzzfeed and the Decline of Journalism

Once upon a time, journalism involved gathering as much information related to some current event as possible. Journalists interviewed people who had firsthand knowledge. Finding and connecting with those sources of information was usually tedious and time-consuming. In many cases, people who had information were not cooperative or forthcoming.

Good journalists also reviewed as much information related to a story as they could get their hands on. Sources of information could include court documents and related articles that had been written previously. Once a journalist had all the information together, he or she would boil it down to the essentials that consumers would need to comprehend what was going on.

Ethical journalists felt a sense of responsibility to get more than one side of a story before putting it into circulation. At the same time, they frequently had deadlines to complete what they were working on. They couldn't always review all the information that was available or talk to all the people involved by the time the deadline hit. In order to avoid getting fired, journalists would put together their articles and stories from the materials they had been able to gather within the allotted time. It's the nature of the business.

In addition to deadline pressures, journalists traditionally want to be the first to get a news story on the record. Being first is frequently referred to as "getting a scoop." Getting scoops is one of the ways journalists build their careers. If newspaper A can get a hot story out a day before newspaper B, newspaper A would generally be regarded as superior. That is, unless they rushed things, cut corners, and published information that was not correct.

Things have changed. It's no longer necessary to interview people, to gather lots of information from lots of places, or to verify information. In a pinch, one source will do just fine, especially if it aligns with the biases and beliefs of a reporter or his or her organization. Writing, rewriting, fact-checking, verifying, rewriting, and editing aren't necessary either. All that old-fashioned stuff is just a big waste of time which could keep an organization from getting a "story" out first.

Regurgitating a document, or a dossier, is much more efficient. Buzzfeed's publication of erroneous and unverified documents without providing context was not journalism. CNN was irresponsible when they passed the bogus story along. The era of fake-alism is upon us. Ironically, the news organizations that engage in it stand to lose their credibility through it.

Buzzfeed's Disclaimer

"A dossier, compiled by a person who has claimed to be a former British intelligence official, alleges Russia has compromising information on Trump. The allegations are unverified, and the report contains errors."

https://www.buzzfeed.com/kenbensinger/these-reports-allege-trump-has-deep-ties-to-russia?utm_term=.fo8x4jYJ4#.cfgxa5ZXa

It appears that two reporters, Ken Bensinger and Miriam Elder, worked on the dossier post along with editor Mark Schoofs.

How many Buzzfeed employees does it take to write a disclaimer? It appears that an article was in the planning stages, but the folks at Buzzfeed had misgivings. Maybe they had a feeling that it wouldn't pan out because they knew they were dealing with a shady operator. However, the story was also too juicy and too perfect for their readership to just set it aside. So, Buzzfeed put the information out there with a disclaimer they could use to get themselves off the hook, so to speak.

A person who has claimed to be? That sounds very reliable. Not somebody with a name. Not a reliable source. Not even someone who spoke on condition of anonymity. A person who claimed to be something in a package of documents that was unverified.

For a look at some real journalism related to the now infamous dossier, check out this article from The Telegraph.

Former MI6 officer Christopher Steele, who produced Donald Trump Russian dossier, 'terrified for his safety' and went to ground before name released.

http://www.telegraph.co.uk/news/2017/01/11/former-mi6-officer-produced-donald-trump-russian-dossier-terrified/

"… the report contains errors." That's like saying "We don't know if it's real and we won't be standing behind it if it's not."

Would it be acceptable in any other business where accuracy matters to present a report that contained errors? Getting the story right isn't easy. Even with softball community news, of which I wrote some, it's hard to get all the details right. Nevertheless, getting the story right is what journalists are supposed to do.

Buzzfeed's suggestion that Americans could make up their own minds about the unverified material in the dossier was ridiculous. How is one supposed to make up his or her mind when the only information available has errors?

Note: On the morning of Friday, January 13th, 2017, The Wall Street Journal published a note from Ben Smith, Editor in Chief of Buzzfeed, to his staff. It was dated January 10th, the night the dossier was published, and it explained the rationale for publishing it.

"We have been chasing specific claims in this document for weeks, and will continue to," Smith wrote.

So, in spite of the fact that two reporters and an editor had been trying to dig a story out of the dossier, and had, apparently, not come up with one, Buzzfeed moved forward and published the dossier anyways. That's very interesting because they apparently did find that the dossier contained some errors. That would have been a red flag to most editors.

Editors generally don't like to use unnamed sources or documents that have not been verified. They don't like sticking their own necks out, or the necks of their organizations, based on unnamed or unverified sources of information. When using an unnamed source, editors are usually very careful to make sure that whatever information they're getting is reliable. Otherwise, when a story based on an unverified source falls apart because the information wasn't accurate, the editor and the organization look bad, the way Ben Smith and Buzzfeed looked.

Why did Ben Smith stick his neck out the way he did? Why did he think that there was enough accurate information in the dossier to publish it, in spite of the fact that his own subordinates had not been able to produce a story out of it? I'd speculate that the dossier catered to his biases and beliefs in the same way that all kinds of fake news caters to the biases and beliefs of audiences. People believe fake news because they want to believe. Even very smart people and people who should know better can be fooled.

Pizzagate: When fake news collides with real life.

According to news sources, a lone gunman, Edgar Welch, went to the Comet Ping Pong Pizza restaurant in Washington D.C. to personally investigate allegations that Hillary Clinton and John Podesta were involved in a child sex ring.

According to a blog called State of the Nation (SOTN), which has posted numerous articles about PIZZAGATE, the scandal involved "ultra-serious criminal activity involving child trafficking, child rape, child torture, child pornography, Satanic ritual child sexual abuse, children snuff films to name but a few."

There's very little information about SOTN on the website. SOTN provides no information about who is involved with the SOTN website at any level. No named reporters, no named editors, no named publisher. The Whois directory, where information about the owners of domain names can sometimes be found, also provided no information about the domain for the website (http://stateofthenation2012.com).

The About page says, "We are about one thing: Accurately portraying the **State of the Nation**. We have no political affiliation. **SOTN** has no other interest except uncovering and presenting the facts. **SOTN** commentary provides a uniquely insightful perspective rarely found anywhere else in alternative news media. **SOTN** strives to feature content that is of the highest journalistic quality."

No evidence has been presented to show that the Pizzagate stories are true. Nevertheless, SOTN and likeminded conspiracy theorists now claim that media organizations are attempting to discredit the Pizzagate stories by labeling them as fake news.

Here are links to a few of the related stories that have appeared in more mainstream media, where the names of the reporters are at the top of the articles and information about the organizations can easily be found.

Death threats, abuse, then a gunman: 'Pizzagate' businesses relive ordeal. The Guardian

https://www.theguardian.com/us-news/2016/dec/06/pizzagate-businesses-washington-threats

How Pizzagate went from fake news to a real problem for a D.C. business. Politifact

http://www.politifact.com/truth-o-meter/article/2016/dec/05/how-pizzagate-went-fake-news-real-problem-dc-busin/

Even the Pizzagate Suspect No Longer Believes the Conspiracy Theory. Esquire

http://www.esquire.com/news-politics/news/a51268/what-is-pizzagate/

'Pizzagate' scare becomes flashpoint in fake news debate. The Hill

http://thehill.com/homenews/administration/308882-pizzagate-scare-becomes-flashpoint-in-fake-news-debate

Here's Everything You Need To Know About The Pizzagate Conspiracy Theory. Daily Wire

http://www.dailywire.com/news/11343/heres-everything-you-need-know-about-pizzagate-aaron-bandler

Can fake news ruin reputations?

An article by health guru David Wolfe about the dangers of Reese's Peanut Butter Cups went viral in March of 2017.

According to the about page on his website (https://www.davidwolfe.com/about/), "David Wolfe is the rock star and Indiana Jones of the superfoods and longevity universe. The world's top CEOs, ambassadors, celebrities, athletes, artists, and the real superheroes of this planet—Moms—all look to David for expert advice in health, beauty, herbalism, nutrition, and chocolate!"

Snopes rates Wolfe's claims about the three dangerous components in Reese's Peanut Butter Cups as mostly false.

http://www.snopes.com/peanut-butter-cups/

And this isn't the first time that Reese's has come under dubious fire. In 2014, a video of maggots in a peanut butter cup went viral. Check out the Snopes article about that.

http://www.snopes.com/food/tainted/reeses.asp

Following the election of Donald Trump in November of 2016, Pepsi CEO Indra Nooyi was quoted as saying that Trump supporters "should take their business elsewhere." That quote apparently originated on a website called Conservative Treehouse and spread quickly. In response to the "news" Trump supporters called for a boycott of Pepsi products. However, it was a fake quote. Indra Nooyi never said it, but that didn't matter. The damage had been done. **Check out coverage from CBS News.**

http://www.cbsnews.com/news/trump-supporters-boycott-pepsico-over-fake-ceo-reports/

In 2014, Rolling Stone published a 9000 word article by Sabrina Rubin Erderly about an alleged gang rape at a University of Virginia Fraternity House.

"The article sparked a national outcry as a shocking example of campus sexual violence, but turned into a journalism scandal when the story's central claims unraveled." Jacob Gershman in the Wall Street Journal.

https://www.wsj.com/articles/rolling-stone-settles-suit-over-retracted-rape-on-campus-article-1492013196

The Rolling Stone article was not true. Among other fake details, Nicole Eramo, Associate Dean of Students at the University of Virginia, was portrayed as an administrator who didn't care about the allegations. Eramo sued and Rolling Stone settled with her in April, 2017.

It takes intelligence and an inquisitive mind to become a good journalist, and Erderly had a good career going as a journalist. However, on this rape story it appears that she was not sufficiently inquisitive. It appears that she accepted what the "victim" was telling her even when it didn't make sense and couldn't be verified. It appears that she wanted to believe. This is how fake news works. Even smart people can be fooled.

Fake news can certainly ruin reputations. It can have an enormous impact on stock values. It can tarnish the reputations of institutions like the University of Virginia as well as the members of the fraternity mentioned in the article.

Consumers of news should be skeptical of anything they see on the internet unless it is from a very trusted source. Remember that even reputable news organizations are being fooled by fake news. Think twice before passing information along.

President Trump declares war on fake news.

One of President Trump's most consistent targets throughout the election season was the media in general and fake news in particular. It was a big part of Trump's schtick. Since his inauguration, he has continued his criticisms. Why would he stop doing what has worked so well for him? President Trump recently called fake news the "enemy of the people." President Trump clearly believes that journalists who produce unfavorable coverage should be treated as enemies.

Trump's dislike for the media is understandable. Many in the media detest Trump and it's obvious. Most of the media were way off in their polling and their prognostications about the election. They said, over, and over, and over that he didn't stand a chance. More recently, the infamous dossier that was published by Buzzfeed has yet to result in any big stories.

Following some unfavorable coverage of the administration in February of 2017, CNN and the New York Times were shut out of a press briefing with White House Press Secretary Sean Spicer. One wonders what will happen next. Will the practice of excluding critical media increase? Will media organizations try to be nicer in order to avoid being excluded? Will someone – perhaps Jimmy Carter – step up to help Trump and the media negotiate for a lasting peace?

Here are a few of the highlights from President Trump's CPAC speech of February 24, 2017.

"I want you to know that we are fighting the fake news."

"They make up sources. They're very dishonest people."

"I'm against the people that make up stories and make up sources."

"There are some terrible dishonest people and they do a tremendous disservice to our country and to our people."

"They're very smart, they're very dishonest, and they're very cunning."

"We're going to do something about them."

Here are a few links to stories about President Trump's CPAC speech.

New York Times: Trump Tears Into the Media at CPAC

https://www.nytimes.com/video/us/politics/100000004953962/trump-tears-into-the-media-at-cpac.html

Washington Post: Donald Trump's CPAC speech proves it: He's totally obsessed with the media

https://www.washingtonpost.com/news/the-fix/wp/2017/02/24/trumps-media-obsessed-cpac-speech-annotated/?utm_term=.65881d80326b

Time: President Trump's CPAC Speech Quickly Turned Into a Media-Bashing Session

http://time.com/4681802/donald-trump-cpac-speech-media/

Chicago Tribune: Trump uses CPAC to blast media, anonymous sources – after White House uses them

http://www.chicagotribune.com/news/nationworld/politics/ct-trump-cpac-20170224-story.html

The Blaze: Trump returns to CPAC; rails against the media

http://www.theblaze.com/news/2017/02/24/trump-returns-to-cpac-rails-against-the-media/

Fox News: Trump Speaks at CPAC: Media Should Not Be Allowed to Use Unnamed Sources

http://insider.foxnews.com/2017/02/24/president-donald-trump-cpac-speech-video-highlights-quotes

CNN: Trump rips media, repeats 'enemy of the people' line

http://money.cnn.com/2017/02/24/media/trump-media-cpac/

Facebook's Plan to Fight Fake News

"We have a responsibility to reduce the spread of fake news on our platform." Adam Mosseri, Facebook Vice President

Facebook is putting in a system for reporting potential fake news stories. Some of those stories will be checked out by Snopes, PolitiFact, and other fine organizations. If a story is fake, it will be labeled as such. So, essentially, there will be warning labels on fake news stories. It appears to be a step in the right direction but there are some serious questions that will need to be addressed.

Who will determine which stories to check out and on what basis? Like news organizations and police departments, fact-checkers have limited resources. It won't be possible to check out each and every lead. There will be some picking and choosing. Like most people, fact-checkers have biases. Will political leanings enter into the selection mix? That's probably inevitable.

How will Facebook label various types of fake news? Satire, hoax news, and deliberate disinformation are three very different things. If I write a piece of satire, which I do from time to time, and label it as such, could my work still be labeled as fake news? I see that as a serious problem.

Newsflash: As I have mentioned previously, fake news is here to stay. It makes lots of money for the people who produce it and for the advertisers who get customers from it. Furthermore, readers and viewers love fake news. Fake news caters to people's biases and beliefs. Some of it is also very entertaining. Many prefer it to real news. That's why people consume so much of it. Facebook's plan is an early step in a complicated endeavor. It will obviously have to be tweaked frequently.

Check out these stories for more information.

Wall Street Journal, Facebook's Fake Fix for Fake News. "Facebook has long insisted that it is neutral about content, and earlier this year it denied reports that the platform censored conservative news. That's looking less credible."

http://www.wsj.com/articles/facebooks-fake-fix-for-fake-news-1481932361

Facebook will start telling you when a story may be fake: Washington Post

https://www.washingtonpost.com/news/the-switch/wp/2016/12/15/facebook-will-start-telling-you-when-a-story-may-be-fake/?utm_term=.4b5d14172b00

Facebook Details Its New Plan To Combat Fake News Stories: NPR

http://www.npr.org/sections/thetwo-way/2016/12/15/505728377/facebook-details-its-new-plan-to-combat-fake-news-stories

Macedonia's fake news industry flourishes: Financial Times

https://www.ft.com/content/333fe6bc-c1ea-11e6-81c2-f57d90f6741a

The Real History of Fake News. Columbia Journalism Review

http://www.cjr.org/special_report/fake_news_history.php

Fake News International to develop Code of Ethics

Note: This is an example of satirical fake news. I originally wrote it as a blog post and it has been one of my most viewed posts. It is absurd to think that people who produce fake news for profit would develop a code of ethics. That's the point of the piece.

Fake News International (FNI) has announced that the organization will develop a formal code of ethics and standards at its annual conference in Macedonia. Jack O'Lanterni, the President of FNI, said, "Fake news provides a valuable service to consumers. Like Jack Nicholson said in that movie, A Few Good Jarheads, although people say they want the truth, the truth is that most people can't handle the truth. What people truly want is news that confirms their beliefs and biases. That's what people get with fake news and that's why they love it."

O'Lanterni went on to say, "Unfortunately, fake news providers have recently come under attack from political leaders throughout the world. She and others claim that fake news is affecting the outcomes of elections and wreaking other forms of havoc on society. Major media establishments, which have been duped time after time by fake news, have also become highly critical of the producers of fake news. It has become clear that in order to avoid losing credibility, creators of fake news must become more accountable and transparent."

Another item on the agenda for the conference will be the establishment of labels to ensure that readers and viewers of fake news understand what they are consuming. O'Lanterni said, "When people read a fake news story, sometimes they don't even realize it. They accept, without question, what's being presented to them. FNI intends to provide fake news creators with guidelines for clearly labeling stories. Whether an article is satire, propaganda, disinformation, or misinformation, consumers need labels at the top so that they won't make the mistake of thinking that what they are reading is true."

Some fake news providers are objecting to the push for ethics. One FNI member, who spoke on condition of anonymity, is organizing a campaign against a code of ethics and standards. "If I wanted to make an honest living, I would have become a journalist or a politician. I make my living by writing interesting and entertaining stories that get people to click on ads," he said. "It's not my fault that people are gullible enough to believe what I write. Ethics and labels aren't going to get people to click on ads, so who needs them? I certainly don't. There are lots of other fake news creators who feel the same way. If FNI moves forward with this, many of us will not be renewing our memberships."

Fake news of an impending apocalypse? Total Eclipse, Mayan Calendar, Y2K, and more.

Doomsday predictions are frequently associated with dates on the calendar, most often at the end of the year or thereabouts. Sometimes apocalypses are expected to accompany phenomena in space like total eclipses, Jupiter aligning with Mars, etc. Consumers love predictions of an apocalypse almost as much as they love celebrity gossip.

For example, December 21st, 2012, was predicted to be an apocalyptic date based on an ancient Mayan calendar. There was great fanfare as the date got closer. No notable events happened that day.

Y2K, January 1, 2000, was the date of another predicted apocalypse. The calendars on much computer software and hardware were not programmed for the year 2000. It was widely anticipated that computers would shut down or malfunction on that date.

- Aircraft which relied on computers would crash.

- Stock markets would cease to function.

- Social security checks would not go out.

Y2K was projected to be the mother of all computer bugs - the end of the world as we knew it. In the years leading up to Y2K, lucrative businesses were built to help other businesses prepare for Y2K. January 1st came and went. Life went on.

People have been predicting end-of-the-world apocalypses for a very long time. Many human beings have a deep-seated belief that something is wrong with the world and that something awful is going to come of that. That's never going to stop. Well, at least not until one of the predictions comes true.

World predicted to end in 2017 thanks to a total solar eclipse hitting America and the UK. The Sun

https://www.thesun.co.uk/news/1728165/world-predicted-to-end-in-2017-thanks-to-a-total-solar-eclipse-hitting-america-and-the-uk/

End of world NEXT YEAR: 'Prophets' warn 2017 will be year of God's vengeance. Daily Sun

http://www.dailystar.co.uk/news/latest-news/545975/end-of-the-world-Gods-vengeance-apocalypse-last-judgement-day-Bible-prophecy

Ten Apocalyptic Movies of 2016 and 2017

http://illusion.scene360.com/movies/101281/apocalyptic-movies-2016-2017/

Every time something in the world changes that groups of people find upsetting, fears of an impending apocalypse are restored. There's certainly no shortage of apocalyptic predictions related to the election of Donald Trump. His talk of improving nuclear capabilities is troubling to many. However, even in the Age of Trump, the odds are that nothing much will come of predictions that an apocalypse is upon us.

"And you shall hear of wars and rumors of wars: see that you be not troubled: for all these things must come to pass, but the end is not yet." Matthew 24:6, KJV

Conclusion

It is becoming increasingly difficult to distinguish what's real and what's fake these days. I'm not just talking about the news.

- Fake memes with photo-shopped images to make people look stupid.

- Fake quotes attributed to people who never said them. Sometimes quotes are combined with photos to portray people like Einstein and Twain saying things they never said.

- Fake heroes who wear military uniforms and decorations they have no business wearing.

- Fake stories being told by people trying to make themselves look good or to look like victims.

- Fake reviews of products and services produced to harm the businesses of competitors.

- Fake illnesses and tragedies intended to raise funds on a GoFundMe page or elsewhere.

- Fake videos of things that never really happened and were staged or edited to promote a political cause.

The list could go on and on. In this day and age, it's no wonder that there's so much fake news to pander to the masses of viewers and readers who are happy to consume it. To reiterate one of my main points, fake news is here to stay. The main reason is that consumers of fake news like it. Indeed, many prefer fake news to real news.

The law of supply and demand dictates that if there is a demand for a product, there will also be a supply of it. Suppliers of fake news are doing well at present and there's no reason to think that the demand for their product is going to decrease.

Professors, politicians, and pundits can lament all they want, but it won't change the fact that most consumers of news prefer to read and view material that confirms what they believe in rather than material that challenges their beliefs. In addition, most people simply don't have the time or the desire to dig deeper or to look at more than one side of any issue. This is the world we are living in.

There will continue to be a percentage of consumers who will take the time to scratch beneath the surface to get a better understanding of the truth about various issues. People who want to understand the truth don't want to be fooled by fake news, regardless of whether it aligns with their beliefs. The more informed a person can become in regard to fake news, the less likely he or she is to be fooled by it.

New fake news circulates every day. The producers of fake news will continue to improve their techniques and their abilities to get clicks and generate web traffic. The best approach to avoid being fooled is to maintain a high level of skepticism about everything you read and view.

The truth is out there. Somewhere. Along with lots of fake news.

Glossary

Many professions have languages of their own that outsiders are not privy to. Journalism and the media are not exceptions. There are words that come up from time to time that outsiders are not familiar with. Here are a few of them, with definitions.

agitprop: agitational propaganda.

anchor: the person on a television news show who reads the news.

backgrounder: an interview with a reporter that is on the record but where the statements cannot be attributed to the source.

bafflegab: jargon intended to confuse rather than to communicate.

byline: the line in a printed story where an author's name is found.

character assassin: one who seeks to destroy a political adversary's reputation.

chilling: adjective implying the inhibition of free speech.

deadline: the date and time by which a reporter must turn in a story to an editor.

disinformation: intentionally false or misleading information that is produced to deceive target audiences.

dope story: leaked information that a reporter publishes as his or her own writing.

facetime: face to face meeting with an important person.

fallout: unexpected negative reaction to a policy or event.

feeding frenzy: intense interest from the media.

fishing expedition: an investigation with no specific objective.

full disclosure: complete release of information.

gag order: rule imposed on the press in some trials to protect a defendant's right to a fair trial.

influence peddler: person who uses his or her influence to obtain government contracts or favors from public officials.

inside baseball: specialized political knowledge.

lead: introduction to a news story.

keeper: a news story held for future use.

leak: release of information through unofficial, and sometimes illegal, channels.

managed news: information produced and distributed to promote the government perspective.

misinformation: false and/or incorrect information.

mudslinging: unsubstantiated charges.

numbers game: misleading use of statistics.

payola: bribes given to radio executives for playing a musician's songs.

plagiarism: the presentation of another person's work as one's own.

plumber: a person who tries to plug information leaks.

premise: a statement that serves as the basis for an argument.

primary source: a source of information that provides the writer or reporter with firsthand material.

propaganda: information used to promote a political cause or point of view.

pundit: political analyst.

pushing the envelope: stretching beyond the boundaries, going to the limit and then some.

readout: a prepared report to the media.

redact: to remove sensitive information from a document prior to publication or distribution.

reputedly: a word that should warn readers or viewers that the story may or may not be true.

sanitize: to delete damaging statements from a document.

secondary sources: articles, reports, etc., written by other people that an author uses for information in his own story or article..

sound bite: snippet of taped news

spin: intentional shading of news to produce a desired political reaction.

surface: to become known.

trial balloon: testing of public reaction to an idea.

witch hunt: hysterical investigation.

Quotes

Some of the things that people in the media say about their profession are interesting. Here are some of the more insightful quotes I've come across over the years. Some of the names may not be familiar to younger consumers, but the ideas are mostly good.

"We are paid to draw a crowd." Phil Donahue

"Reporters are like crabs in a barrel. When one gets up, others pull him down." Jack Anderson

"We're not always as conscious as we should be about the emotional litter we leave in our wake." Peter Jennings

"The fact that a man is a newspaper reporter is evidence of some flaw of character." Lyndon Johnson

"The medium is the message." Marshall McLuhan

"Monopoly is a terrible thing till you have it." Rupert Murdoch

"There is no such thing as objectivity. Any reporter who tells you he's objective is lying to you." Linda Ellerbee

"In America the press rules the country. It rules its politics, its religion, its social practice." Edward W. Scripps

"We look for and hope for a rally bad character to pursue because it can do wonders for our careers." Brit Hume

"Practice whatever the big truth is so you can say it in forty seconds on camera." Newt Gingrich

"We journalists always deal with partial information and know less than we should. We never have as much time as we need." David Broder

"And that's the way it was." Walter Cronkite

"The newspaper is a moral force second only to the church. It is a political power superior to the parties. It's an instrument of justice coequal with the courts." William Randolph Hearst

"For the most part, we do not see first, then define. We define first and then see." Walter Lippman

"With the instrument of radio, you can make public opinion. Perhaps even conquer a country." Joseph Goebbels

"Our republic and its press will rise or fall together." Joseph Pulitzer

"Get your facts first, and then you can distort them as you please." Mark Twain

"Four hostile newspapers are more to be feared than a thousand bayonets." Napoleon

"As long as America continues to be a free country, you will have a lot of bad journalists writing a lot of garbage." Ted Koppel

"In Hollywood we learn about life only from each other's movies." Frank Capra

"People are more readily manipulated through images than just with words." Jeanne Kirkpatrick

"We are the ones that determine what people's attitudes are. It's in our hands." Ted Turner

"A modern revolutionary group heads for the television station." Abbie Hoffman

"In the future everyone will be famous for fifteen minutes." Andy Warhol

"What draws the press is conflict, corruption, and scandal." Bill Moyers

"Show me a man who thinks he's objective, and I'll show you a man who's deceiving himself." Henry Luce

"There is no substitute for circulation." William Randolph Hearst

"The press is the enemy." Richard Nixon

"With the stroke of a pen, a political cartoonist can affect public policy." Gerald Ford

"What concerns me as much as anything is the rush to judgment, with guilt assumed and extenuating circumstance rarely reported." Tom Brokaw

"...even the least informed of the people have learned that nothing in a newspaper is to be believed." Thomas Jefferson

"It takes much more time to dig into a story on your own than it does simply to match what you know your competition is doing." Ted Koppel

"In the old days, they had the rack. Now they have the press." Oscar Wilde

"We don't heave nearly enough accountability in this profession." Frank Sesno

About Danny Murphy

Danny Murphy is a writer and humorist from Jacksonville, Florida. He performed standup comedy for several years in venues from nightclubs to churches. Danny won several joke contests, including Comedy Central's Don't Quit Your Day Job Contest. He has acted in films and commercials and he has been the host of a weekly radio show.

Danny's published work includes hundreds of articles for periodicals such as The Florida Times-Union, The Wittenburg Door, National Business Employment Weekly, and Onyx. He has also written numerous ebooks including Facebook Anonymous, The Narcissus Code, Murphy's Law Breaker, and Humor 101: How to tell jokes for power, prestige, profit, and personal fulfillment.

Check out Danny's Amazon page. https://www.amazon.com/Danny-Murphy/e/B005JVA6U4/ref=dp_byline_cont_ebooks_1

Danny also worked for a social services agency for over a decade, handling media relations, P.R., and written communications. He has done similar work for several business clients including a chiropractor, a performing arts center, and others. If you need content for your blog, website, newsletter, annual report, or other literature, he can provide it.

If you need an entertaining speaker for an event about fake news, or to lighten things up in an informative way for an event that's not directly connected to fake news, Danny can help. To see what Danny can do for you and your organization, send him a message.

Danny@DannyMurphyAuthor.com

Other books by Danny Murphy

Humor 101: How to tell jokes for power, prestige, profit, and personal fulfillment

Revised and updated in 2014, Humor 101 is a self-improvement guide for people who want to tell jokes effectively. You may be a public speaker seeking to improve your Likeability Quotient (LQ) during your opening. You may be a manager or business owner who occasionally has to make a presentation. You may have dreamed of being a standup comedian, like most people, but never found a way to work it out. Or you may just want to get better at telling jokes because you know there's something very funny deep inside you that's going to die a tragic death if you don't figure out how to set it free. Humor 101 will help.

The Narcissus Code: Coming soon to a device near you.

Jonah Redthorn is a freelance writer and photographer who produces puff articles for magazines. It's not the career he envisioned. In college, he aspired to become a hard-hitting investigative journalist. Holistic Health Magazine sends him to cover the release of Narcissus, a new app developed by Dr. Adam Arturo Nova. He is the visionary author of Ultimate Self and Nurture Your Inner Narcissist, two bestsellers in self-help.

Nova plans to use churches as part of his distribution network. L.A. megachurches like Colossal Community Church, The Fabulous Fellowship, and Enormous Empire Network are ideal. He makes them an offer that's hard to refuse. After Nova hires Christine White, Jonah's sweet girlfriend, Narcissus turns her into an online temptress. Redthorn digs deeper. Scratching the shiny surface of Narcissus, he discovers that darkness lurks beneath.

Zeke Thomas, retired rodeo star and the pastor of Sunset Destiny Church, was a protégé of Nova's. He wants the world to learn the truth about Narcissus. Lucy Furman, Nova's alluring assistant, would prefer to prevent that.Can Christine be rescued? Will Pastor Zeke live long enough to tell his story? Can Dr. Nova and Narcissus be stopped? Will Jonah Redthorn answer the call and step up to bring the truth to light?

Facebook Anonymous: A Tale of Addiction

Candace Crush started out as a casual Facebook user. It wasn't long before she became a full-blown addict. "I craved the likes. Then I needed the likes. Then I couldn't get enough of the likes."

What she didn't realize was that the likes were triggering releases of dopamine in her brain. "I posted more and more pictures. However, no matter how many people liked a picture, it was never enough. I wanted the same high that I felt the first time one of my photos became popular. The harder I tried to get that buzz, the further away it seemed to be."

Facebook Anonymous is the comical, and occasionally harrowing, story of one young woman's descent into Facebook addiction. Candace Crush is on the verge of losing her job and her family. She stays logged in even while driving. After plowing into a salon at a strip mall, she is still in denial that she has a problem.

It's her third offense for texting while driving, making her a habitual offender. Judge Killjoy gives her a difficult choice. Candace Crush can either lose her driver's license or go to Facebook Anonymous.

To see samples from these books and others, check out Amazon's Danny Murphy Page.

http://www.amazon.com/Danny-Murphy/e/B005JVA6U4

Made in the USA
Lexington, KY
12 July 2017